D1613609

Teen Fathers

Getting Involved

By Julie K. Endersbe, MEd

Consultant:
William J. Doherty, PhD
Professor, Department of Family Social Science
University of Minnesota

Perspectives on Healthy Sexuality

LifeMatters
an imprint of Capstone Press
Mankato, Minnesota

LifeMatters books are published by Capstone Press
818 North Willow Street • Mankato, Minnesota 56001
http://www.capstone-press.com

Printed in the United States of America

Library of Congress Cataloging-in-Publication Data
Teen fathers: getting involved / by Julie Endersbe.
    p. cm. — (Perspectives on healthy sexuality)
Includes bibliographical references and index.
Summary: Discusses problems and dilemmas faced by teenage males when they become fathers and identifies options and solutions available to them.
ISBN 0-7368-0269-X (book). — ISBN 0-7368-0293-2 (series)
1. Teenage fathers Juvenile literature. [1. Teenage fathers.]
I. Title. II. Series: Endersbe, Julie. Perspectives on healthy sexuality.
HQ756.7.E54 2000
306.874´2—dc21   99-29762
                    CIP

Staff Credits
Anne Heller, editor; Adam Lazar, designer; Heidi Schoof, photo researcher

Photo Credits
Cover: The Stock Market/©Ariel Skelley
FPG International/©Mike Malyszko, 57; ©Jim Whitmer, 6
International Stock/©Laurie Bayer, 33; ©Bob Firth, 42; ©Willie Holdman, 35
PNI/ ©Digital Vision, 29, 39
Unicorn Stock Photos/©Eric R. Berndt, 21, 49; ©Joel Dexter, 26; ©Tommy Dodson, 47, 58; ©Wayne Floyd, 14; ©B.W. Hoffman, 8; ©Martha McBride, 50; ©Jim Shippee, 40
Uniphoto Picture Agency/©Bob Daemmrich, 13
Visuals Unlimited/©Jeff Greenberg, 19

A 0 9 8 7 6 5 4 3 2 1

Table of Contents

Chapter Overview

Young men deal with many different emotions during a pregnancy. The most common are feelings of joy, nervousness, and denial.

It is important to confirm, or be sure about, a pregnancy at a local clinic or hospital.

Fathers can provide support to their pregnant partner.

Fathers can learn about what a woman goes through while she is pregnant.

Chapter 1

Teen Pregnancy—
Whose Problem Is It?

Many people believe teen pregnancy is a female problem.
However, it's also a male problem. A pregnancy means some big
changes in a young man's life. He must deal with many mixed
emotions. He also must make hard decisions. The role a father
plays is important. It affects the rest of his child's life.

> Me and Tamisha have dated for six
> months. She's been actin' all strange lately.
> I can't please her no matter what I do. Last night she told me
> we're gonna have a baby. I can't believe it. I dated a girl for a
> while before Tamisha, and we never got pregnant. I can't
> believe I'm gonna be a daddy.
>
> **Ronnie, Age 17**

Dealing With the Emotions

Many young men feel excited about becoming a father. They may be in love with the mother. Having babies is a natural way to show their love. Some young men feel parenting is a step toward manhood. Others want to pass on their family name. A baby allows them to do this.

The most common feeling for teen fathers, however, is nervousness. Many young men do not feel prepared to be a parent. They may still feel like children themselves. They might not have a good job to support a baby. Most teen fathers have not even finished high school.

Denial is another strong emotion for teen fathers. Some young men deny they are the father. Some blame the mother. They don't feel ready to be a parent. Some young men may even ignore their pregnant partner. They may try to run away from the problem.

Most of the information you read about teen pregnancy applies to young women.
   Teen fathers aren't included in the statistics for many reasons. They don't get pregnant.
   A teen father can't be seen unless he is with his baby. Teen fathers are invisible to most people.

Are You Positive?

It is important to confirm, or be sure, that the woman is definitely pregnant. There are several ways to be sure. You can buy a kit at a store. A kit is a fast and cheap way to know. Positive or negative results show up in minutes. Next, you should confirm the pregnancy at a clinic. Future prenatal visits to the clinic can be set up. These visits happen before the birth. They allow a doctor to check the health of mother and baby.

A teen dad can be a partner in the pregnancy. He can help the mother have a healthy pregnancy. For examplc, he can help the mom get to appointments on time. He can make healthy meals for the mom. He can take walks with the mom.

Many teen fathers want to be good dads. They may choose to quit unhealthy habits. They might stop smoking. They may quit drinking or doing drugs. They might try not to get so angry that they lose control. These changes show support to the mother and the unborn child.

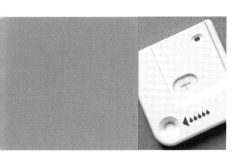

Maria and I were both heavy drinkers when she got pregnant. We would go out four or five nights a week and party. We always were getting ourselves drunk.

Miguel, Age 19

I was raised with no dad around. Maria's parents were both drunks. We knew we had to do it differently. Her doctor gave us the name of a chemical health counselor. He's been great for us. It's not easy. But we've been clean for three months.

The Effects of Pregnancy

A woman's body changes during pregnancy. She may have intense mood swings. She may be calm one moment. The next moment she may be angry. The mother may feel tired or have an upset stomach. She may lose her desire to eat. Some pregnant women seem like different people to those who know them.

Researchers do not know how many teen males become dads each year. Many birth certificates do not name the father. Most birth certificates that do name the father don't list his age.

One in every 15 men fathers a child while he is a teenager.

Fast
Fact

A teen father can give emotional support to his partner. It is important to understand how her body is changing. Hormone activity increases during pregnancy. Hormones are chemicals in the mother's body that help the baby grow. They also affect the mother physically and emotionally. The father needs to learn what is happening to the mother. It will help him provide support.

Points to Consider

Why do people believe teen pregnancy is a female problem?

What emotions do young men feel when they find out about a pregnancy?

How can young men support their pregnant partners?

What would you say to a friend who wants to leave his pregnant girlfriend?

Chapter Overview

The mother has sole physical and legal custody of the baby if the parents are unmarried.

A father must establish paternity to become the legal father. In many states, a form can be signed at the hospital.

A father has many responsibilities. He can provide emotional and physical support to the mother. He can responsibly pay child support. He also can find ways to support himself.

Teen fathers may be forced to deal with issues from their past. Young fathers need to make thoughtful decisions. This includes the type of dad they want to become.

Chapter 2

A Father's Rights and Responsibilities

Married couples assume the husband is the biological father. Almost 80 percent of births to teens, however, happen outside of marriage. An unmarried father has few rights. Unmarried fathers who want rights must sign forms to become the legal father. This is called establishing paternity. Each state or province in North America has a program to help fathers establish paternity.

The Recognition of Parentage is a form that can be signed at the hospital. Sometimes it is called the Declaration of Parentage. It is a legal document. Teens should not sign the form unless they are sure they are the father.

A father benefits from being a legal father.

- He can see the child's school and medical records.
- He has the right to ask the court for custody of the child.
- He can ask the court for visitation rights.

A child benefits from having a legal father.

- The child may receive Social Security, military, health care, and inheritance benefits.
- The child gets help from child support payments.
- The child knows the medical history of his or her father.

When Mai got pregnant, we were really surprised. We only had intercourse once. **Blong, Age 17** You are expected to marry if you get pregnant in the Laotian community. I didn't want Mai to be shamed. But I was not ready to get married. I guess I wasn't ready to be a dad either.

I signed the Recognition of Parentage form at the hospital when the baby was born. Mai and the baby live with her parents. I take care of the baby on the weekends when Mai works. Sometimes I wish the baby lived at my house all the time. I would have to go to court for physical custody, though.

The courts don't seem to like fathers too much. The law gives the mom full custody when a baby is born and the mom isn't married. The mom gets to decide on everything. She decides where the baby lives and the name, too. I'm glad I am the baby's legal father. Now at least I have some rights, too.

Establishing Custody

Unmarried women have sole physical custody of their baby. They also have legal custody. Therefore, it is important that the father be legally identified. The father has more rights when paternity is established.

Some people go to court to decide who is the legal father. A judge reviews information to decide who is the biological father. Blood is taken from the father and compared with the baby's blood. Biological fathers have certain markers in their blood that match markers in the baby's blood. A father can request custody of his baby more easily once paternity is legal. He can also request visitation privileges.

Child Support

Child support issues also are decided in court. Fathers are expected to pay support if they are not living with the mother and child. This is also true for mothers not living with their children. Child support is determined by figuring a percentage of a person's total income. Each state or province has rules for the amount of payments. Some employers take child support money from fathers' paychecks.

Child support is about more than just money. A father has many other responsibilities. He should first become the legal father. He also should communicate with the mother of the baby. He and the mother can share their feelings and compromise. He can play with and care for the baby. He can help around the house. He can wash clothes. He may buy groceries. He can even provide quiet time for the mother to sleep. Those actions all help the baby, too.

Young Teens and Their Fathers

Many young children today are raised without their fathers at home. Young fathers might have to work hard to be the father they never had. They can establish paternity. They can try to share custody of their children. They can choose to be active in the life of their children, even if their own fathers weren't.

Teen fathers also can help themselves. They can offer to baby-sit another young child. This helps them to practice parenting. New dads can enroll in parenting classes. Some new fathers look for support groups to help them become better dads.

Many experts suggest that young dads find a caring adult to talk with. This person can provide support to the teen father. Fathering is a tough job at any time in life. Teen fathering is more difficult. Young men who can find support for themselves are better fathers.

Points to Consider

What are two different ways a father can establish paternity?

How might you find support for yourself if you became a parent?

How does a male's relationship with his own father affect his ability to parent?

At what point in your own life will you be ready to parent? What skills are needed to be a good parent?

Chapter Overview

The news of a pregnancy can be difficult to share. Parents and relatives need time to consider the news.

Young fathers may need to work on being included as a parent.

A change occurs with the birth of a baby. Some young fathers feel alone, or shut out from their old life.

It is important to have a good support system. Family and friends can serve this role.

Chapter 3

Dealing With Your Family and Your Community

I was speechless when Sheila told me she was pregnant. I remember asking her, "Are you hungry? Let's go get a pizza." I thought about college and losing my scholarship. I thought about my own dad never being around. I thought it would never happen to me. Then I thought about my mom. She would be crushed. She worked hard to raise me. She didn't want me to have a baby really young like she did. I didn't know how I could tell my mom about this.

Paul, Age 18

Dealing with your family can be tough. It is important to share the news of a pregnancy as soon as you can.

- Be honest.
- Be timely. Sharing the news early will give you more time to make your decisions.
- Share the news together. A partner's support is important.
- Be thoughtful. You know your parents best. Think about how, when, and where you should share the news.

Telling the Families

A teenage pregnancy is not easy news to share. Many families may not receive the news well. Parents may feel their young son's future is lost. Adult parents might have plans for their son's future. They may grieve the news. They might say hurtful things. Some may not know what to say.

News of a pregnancy can bring mixed responses from the young mother's family. They may blame the father. Her parents may reject the teen father or refuse to allow him in the house. He may be kept from daily routines after the baby is born. Sometimes young fathers must work hard to be included as a parent.

Support from family and friends is an important part of raising a child. In time they may give a teen father the support he needs from them. Time helps people deal with difficult situations.

Adult parents can provide support in many ways. They can listen without blaming. This is an important first step. Some parents provide a safe place for the teen parents to live. They can encourage the young couple to finish school. They can encourage the couple to complete job training. These are good steps for teens to take in order to live independently. Finishing school and job training will help the parents and baby in the long run.

My friends and I partied all night when **Emerson, Age 17**
I found out I was gonna be a daddy.
They were slapping my back, saying, "You're a man, now." I
told them I really loved Deziree. I said we were going to keep
the baby. They were like, "No way . . . leave while you can!
You don't want to be tied down!"

I knew being a daddy would change my life. But my dad was
always there for me. I saw what it did to my friends not to
have their dads around. It's my baby. I'm gonna be a good dad.

Friendships Change

Teen fatherhood affects your friendships. Your social life changes.
It is hard to attend dances and parties. You have to think about a
new baby. You may be too tired to do social things. Your friends
may quit calling or asking you to take part in activities or
gatherings. Many new fathers feel shut out and alone.

It is important to keep good friendships. Young dads need breaks
from parenting. Young mothers do, too. Good parents try to be
balanced. They know when the other person needs a break and
offer it. Parents' breaks are healthy for the baby. Babies are not
safe when their parents are angry and frustrated.

Who are the people in your life to whom you can go for support? Here are some ideas for building your support system.

1. Make a three-column chart. Put your name at the top of the page.

2. List the names of people you can't imagine living without in the first column.

3. In the second column, write down the friends and relatives who almost made the first list.

4. In the last column, list the people and groups with whom you are involved. This might be athletic teams, youth groups, or coworkers.

5. Think of one person who you could add to each list. Write the name down. Then ask yourself what is one more thing you can do to improve that relationship.

6. Commit to building your support system.

Feeling Left Out

A teen father can feel shut out from his old life. Teachers and coaches may keep you from opportunities. Other teens at school may label you. It becomes clear who your friends really are. Clothes and cars may seem less important. Friends who care and who support you become valuable.

Pregnancy is difficult news for teens to share with others. Many young couples prolong the news. Others believe telling the truth is a good thing. It is a chance for your parents to be supportive. It is a chance for you to build a good support system. It helps to find a trusted friend who listens and encourages you to talk. Finally, it is a chance to be honest.

Points to Consider

Describe what a teen father goes through emotionally and socially during a pregnancy.

Why is sharing the news of a pregnancy so difficult?

Why is it important for new parents to have a good support system?

Name two ways your friends may respond to the news that you will be a parent.

Chapter Overview

Good parents need skills to raise healthy children. Many resources help to build parenting skills. They include schools, agencies, doctors, family, and friends.

Skills for fatherhood can be built through family living classes. Help also comes from clinics, family, friends, and neighbors.

A father's behavior affects the mother and fetus during pregnancy.

Chapter 4

Training for Fatherhood

I was the youngest in my family and was never around kids much. I didn't know what to do with them. My daughter, Anna Maria, was born when I was 17. I didn't even know how to hold her. My girlfriend taught me how to change her diaper and stuff.

Guillermo, Age 19

One of my teachers told me about a parenting class. I could take it in school, so I signed up for it. This year I was recruited to drive a bus for Head Start. Every day, I work for at least an hour in the classroom, too. The kids really like me. They yell, "Hi, Mr. G!" when they see me. I've learned so much about kids. It's really helped me be a good dad to Anna Maria.

"One of the most important things we can do to prepare men to be active, involved, nurturing fathers would be to get them involved with babies and young children before they become fathers."
—William Doherty, 1998

Good parenting requires many skills. This may include learning about child development and budgets. It includes knowing about first aid and nutrition and finding helpful resources. When an unplanned pregnancy happens, you need these skills right away. It takes planning and effort to learn these skills.

Learning About Fatherhood

A young man does not carry a baby, but he is a part of the pregnancy. He is a partner. Healthy relationships are based on partnerships. These partnerships are two-way streets. Each person gives and receives. You may receive less at certain times and more at other times. In the end, it should even out.

The following teen fathers describe how they made teen pregnancy a positive thing. They worked on their weaknesses. They also built on their strengths. This helped them to be successful fathers.

I was a junior in high school when my girlfriend got pregnant. My dad was the one who really guided me. He reminded me of all the good things I'd done in my life. He helped me get ready to take responsibility. Sometimes I still get really frustrated. It is hard to be a good father. My dad seems to know exactly what to say.—Zach, age 18

Successful Teen Fathers

I quit school when Cherille was born. I couldn't handle the structure. I had my GED within three months. Then I started working with my uncle. He does upholstery. I'm pretty good at making these old chairs look new. It's like on-the-job training, only my uncle is more flexible. I've made enough money to rent an apartment with Cherille's mom. Cherille has been sick a few times. My uncle always lets me off work to take her to the clinic.—Charles, age 19

My mom made me sign up for a parenting class. This was after she found out my girlfriend and I were gonna have a baby. At first I didn't like it, but it's been an okay class. I think it will help me a lot with the baby. I was also assigned a mentor through my Young Father's group. He's a cool guy. His name is Evan. He raised five boys! I'm feeling less nervous about the baby coming.—Randy, age 16

Building Support

Sometimes young men are reluctant to ask for help. However, there are many people who want to help. Finding and building support makes being a young father easier.

Make a list of all the people and supports in your life. Schools offer family living classes. Schools also have counselors. Try a class or a visit with a counselor to see if you like it.

Local clinics teach about methods that prevent pregnancy from happening. An obstetrician, or woman's doctor, can provide information on birthing classes. The clinic can share information about nutrition and exercise.

Family, friends, and neighbors are also resources. They can help provide names of good doctors. They also can help provide guidance to young parents.

Advice From Teens

It helps to practice being a dad. The following activities can help:

Baby-sit. My sister was always asked to baby-sit, but I never was. It would have been good for me.—Jamal, age 18

Take parenting classes. My school has a great class on parenting. We worked with babies twice a week. I learned how to diaper and feed a baby. I learned a lot because I got to do it, not watch someone else do it.—Enrique, age 19

Hang out with kids. There are a ton of kids in my neighborhood. Every summer we start our day with a game of baseball. Everyone plays—even the little five-year-olds. I've learned how to solve a lot of problems with kids. —William, age 17

Find good father role models. I never knew my dad. But my Uncle Gary worked hard to be a dad to me. He helped my art skills. I always had art supplies around, thanks to him. He also encouraged me to go to art school. I look up to him like a father.—Benjamin, age 20

Communicate and compromise. My parents always fought. I never learned how to listen or talk about things. My girlfriend has taught me how to listen. She doesn't like power struggles. I am learning how to work through things in a good way.—LuWayne, age 18

Many pregnant teens do not receive good prenatal care. Babies born to teen mothers are more likely to weigh too little. This can lead to childhood health problems. These children are more likely to be hospitalized than are those born to older mothers.

The Father's Role in Prenatal Care

The mother's choices affect her unborn child. Mothers who smoke while pregnant give birth to babies who weigh too little. Even small amounts of alcohol can affect the fetus, or unborn baby. Drugs like cocaine, crack, or heroin are also very harmful to the fetus. Babies are born addicted to the drug.

Researchers believe the male partner influences the health of the mother. Fathers who use alcohol and other drugs sometimes pressure their pregnant partner to use. A father's healthy choices can affect the pregnant woman's decisions. For example, she may be more willing to avoid drugs if he does. Mothers also are more likely to seek early prenatal care when fathers are supportive.

A father plays a major role during a pregnancy. He can influence the mother's healthy decisions. He can give positive encouragement. He also can model healthy behaviors. He and his partner can work together to have a healthy pregnancy.

Points to Consider

Describe three resources in your life that provide support.

How is a parenting relationship like a partnership?

How do the father's decisions affect the mother and her baby?

What steps can a father take to make sure his partner has a healthy pregnancy?

Chapter Overview

Fathers play an important role during birth. They can coach or model breathing exercises. They can offer positive words. They can simply massage the mother's back during labor and delivery.

Some mothers experience postpartum depression after birth. Fathers can take a more active role during this time.

A father's attachment with the baby begins immediately. Fathers who are involved in the baby's daily care build a positive attachment.

Babies learn trust when fathers listen to them. Fathers comfort the baby when they talk gently during routine parts of the day.

Chapter 5

The Birth

In the past, hospitals did not allow fathers in the labor and delivery room. Fathers stayed in a waiting room until the baby was born. Today, hospitals encourage fathers to take an active role during the birth of a baby. This includes teen fathers.

It can be hard for a father to watch a birth. He may feel helpless, but he is not helpless. In fact, a father can do several important things. Birthing classes teach a father how to coach the mother. A father's positive words encourage the mother during labor and delivery. Also, back massage and companionship help the mother feel supported.

A baby's cry means many things. When parents respond to a baby's cries, the baby learns to trust its parents. Crying may mean:

- The baby's diaper needs to be changed.
- The baby is hungry and needs to be fed.
- The baby is tired and needs to sleep.
- The baby may be getting sick if he or she feels warm.

The mother may experience postpartum depression after delivery. This condition causes the mother to feel sad and hopeless. It can last for a few days or weeks after delivery. It happens to some women because of the hormonal changes. Mothers may not be able to parent as well during the depression. A father can deal with the depression if he understands the symptoms. Many fathers take a more active role during this depression. Postpartum depression does go away.

Baby Care

One of the most important parts of baby care is communication. Babies like gentle talk. They learn to recognize their father's voice. Dads can cuddle new babies and look into their eyes. Newborns cannot focus on a face. This takes several weeks. Soon they learn to know their father's face. This communication helps dads and babies to grow close.

Baby care includes much more. Some people say new parents do three things. First, they change diapers. Second, they feed the baby. Finally, they sleep when the baby sleeps. Parenting is much more rewarding than this. These three events, however, occupy most of the baby's early months.

Diapers and Feeding

Newborns go through about a dozen diapers a day. The diapers must be changed often. That helps to keep the baby happy. Frequent changing prevents diaper rash, which is painful to a baby. Parents can purchase medicine to heal the rash. Parents should avoid using baby powder on the baby's bottom. Too much powder can affect how the baby breathes.

Feeding time can be a special time for baby and dad. Many mothers choose to breast-feed. This means dad cannot feed the baby. As the baby grows, however, dad will have more chances to help feed. In the meantime, dad can hold and talk to the baby so they grow close. Dad can bottle-feed and burp the baby.

Quiet feeding times can lead to sleeping time. Babies need quiet time to sleep and nap. Babies who live in noisy areas have a harder time learning to sleep. Regular sleeping patterns are good for babies. Patterns provide a stable time for babies to grow and develop. Routines do not happen overnight. They also may not work everyday. Still, a routine is good for babies if parents can use one.

At a Glance

Babies need to see a doctor many times, even when they are not sick. This is the suggested schedule for baby's doctor visits:

2 weeks	Newborn checkup
2, 4, 6 months	Physical exam and immunizations
10 months	Physical exam, blood work, and immunizations
15 months	Physical exam and immunizations
2 years	Physical exam
3½ years	Physical exam and vision screening

Doctor Visits

Regular doctor visits help to keep a baby healthy. Doctors check whether babies are growing and developing normally. Many fathers build good relationships with their baby's doctor. Fathers can ask the baby's doctor any questions they have.

All children need immunizations, or vaccinations. These shots prevent many childhood diseases. Children should have five immunizations in their first year and a half. The schedule for these visits is shown above. The first round of shots should happen at two months. Immunizations are required before a child starts kindergarten. Preventive care ensures that a baby is not at risk for disease.

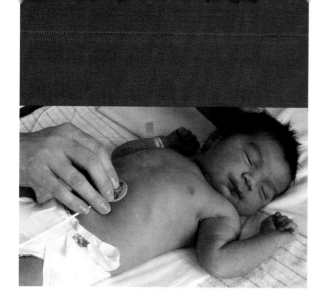

Points to Consider

How does postpartum depression affect the father?

Name three things a father can do for his baby daily.

What kinds of risks would there be if babies never visited a doctor?

Why are dads important to their children?

Chapter Overview

Teen dads can support families in many ways. They can pay child support. They can finish school and complete job training.

The government controls child support. The government tries to make sure parents pay child support.

Fathers who work often get health insurance. Their children can be covered through their insurance.

Babies are expensive. Food, diapers, clothes, and furniture cost a lot. Parents should learn how to budget their money.

Chapter 6

The Costs of Raising a Baby

Babies are expensive. They need medical care. They get sick and need medicine. They need special foods when they are young. They go through a lot of diapers. Babies depend on their parents to keep them safe. It takes money to keep babies safe and healthy.

Supporting a Family

Many teen fathers do not live with the mother and baby. It is hard to share family expenses when you don't live together. Some teen dads give money through child support payments. Some states don't make teen fathers pay until they are 18 years old. It is hard for fathers to pay child support if they don't have a job.

The U.S. Census Bureau records how much money people make. This chart shows about how much money people make in a lifetime. It is based on their level of education.

No high school diploma	$609,000
High school diploma	$821,000
Some college	$993,000
Associate's degree	$1,062,000
Bachelor's degree	$1,421,000
Master's degree	$1,619,000
Doctorate	$2,142,000
Professional (doctor, lawyer)	$3,013,000

Finding a Job

Job training is an important step toward supporting your baby. Some fathers attend college. A college education provides a chance to earn a living wage. Colleges offer two-year or four-year programs.

Vocational training is another choice for young fathers. Classes help people learn jobs like computer programmer, mechanic, or plumber. Some people start these classes while they are in high school. They are released from school early to attend.

Some teen fathers do not do well in school. These young men may choose on-the-job training. This happens when a person learns a job while doing it. For example, you can learn to be a cook by working in a restaurant. You can earn a salary while you learn.

Paying Child Support

A job application asks people if they must pay child support. Employers take money out of each paycheck for child support. For example, a father's payroll check may be for $100. Child support payments may reduce the check to $80.

The amount taken from a check depends on two things. First, it depends on how much money the person makes. Second, it depends on how many children the person has to support. Some fathers may pay as little as 16 percent of their income. Other fathers pay half of their income to support their children.

Some teen fathers who have jobs choose not to pay child support. The government tries to find parents who don't pay. It can keep extra money from a parent's paycheck. It can take away a car or freeze a bank account. It also can keep money won in a lottery. It is important that parents make an effort to pay child support.

Health Insurance

Many companies offer health insurance to employees. Health insurance protects a family from costly medical bills. It pays most of an employee's medical bills. The employee pays the part that the insurance doesn't cover. Fathers can insure their children when they have health benefits.

I work for a small plastics company. I **Chieu, Age 19** started out doing assembly work. My boss saw how hard I worked. He gave me more responsibility. It was hard to leave my job when my daughter got sick. She had to go to the hospital three times. Each emergency room visit cost more than $1,000. My company has good health insurance. I only had to pay $40 each time. I am glad I can provide this for my family.

Daily Expenses

Babies seem to grow every day. They grow out of clothes. They need more food. They need a lot of clean diapers. Basic supplies for a baby cost about $2,000 for the first year. This is for the most basic things. New clothes and furniture are more expensive.

Parents can save money by finding bargains. They may go to garage sales. Second-hand stores also sell used furniture and clothes. Babies grow so fast that they don't wear out clothes. Used clothing and furniture are good choices for families on a budget.

You may have to live at home while raising your baby. It can be hard to deal with your own parents. You can try to:

- Set boundaries with your parents.
- Make sure you have your own private area.
- Not expect your parents to do all the work.
- Be responsible.
- Talk with your parents—communication is important.
- Make sure individuals understand their roles.

The cost of housing is a large part of a budget. Rent for an apartment or other housing can be expensive. Parents also must decide if they are going to live together. Some states require a teen mother to live at home. She must stay at home until age 18 if she gets public money. Welfare laws change often. It is a good idea to understand those laws in your state or province.

Many teens raise their babies at home. They get some support from their parents. This is an affordable choice for them. It can raise other problems, however. Sometimes a young parent acts more like a kid. Adult parents may still treat teen parents like children. It is hard for teens to move into a more responsible role. This is especially true when adults don't think a teen has acted like an adult.

Keeping a Budget

The average total cost of a baby's first year is about $22,000. This includes housing costs. It also includes daily expenses and medical bills. In addition, young fathers need food and clothing for themselves. They need a car or a bus pass to get to school or work. This costs more money.

A budget is a good way to keep track of money. Young parents need to learn how to budget. They need good jobs. They need an education. These are hard needs to balance. Yet they are important to the wellness of a family. Most social service agencies can offer help with a budget. School guidance counselors also might be able to help.

Points to Consider

Which do you think is more important for a young father: to finish high school or to start working right away? Why?

How do child support payments work?

What can the government do to enforce child support payments?

What are the benefits of good job training?

List five expenses of raising a child. What steps would you take to meet these expenses?

Chapter Overview

Parents who work together as a team put their child first.

Fathers keep feelings about the mother separate from feelings about their child. They keep the child out of arguments.

Parents who care about children value fathers. They recognize the special role a father plays in a child's life. They encourage the father's involvement.

A father needs to understand child development. It will help him understand how his baby grows and changes. This can help him understand the baby's behavior.

Chapter 7

Working Together

The teen birth rate was high in the 1950s. Many teens married when a pregnancy occurred. This did not solve the teen pregnancy problem. Some young couples were not ready for marriage. They had enough stress just being parents.

Half of all children born today will spend part of their childhood in a single-parent home.

Today, it is less common for teens to marry when they get pregnant. Some families include one parent. A parent who raises a child alone faces many difficulties. No other adult is around for daily support. There is only one income. No one is around to give the parent a break. Raising a child alone puts a lot of pressure on one person.

Single parenting is not impossible. It is simply more difficult. It is also harder on the child.

Parents Can Work as a Team

Teen parents must make hard decisions. They must decide how they will parent together. Few teen parents marry each other. In fact, fewer than one in four marry. Often teen parents don't live in the same home. Parenting may be done in two different homes. Young couples can still parent together. Children are healthier and better adjusted if the parents work together.

Teen parents may share custody of the child. Sometimes only one parent has primary custody. That parent is responsible for decisions about the child.

It helps some couples to view parenting as a business deal. This works best when the mother and father are not dating each other anymore. They work together as business partners. They use their strengths and skills to raise a healthy child together.

Putting Children First

Good fathers put their children first. This does not mean they let children do whatever they want. It means they put the needs of the children above their own needs. Parents make sacrifices. For example, a father may give up an expensive motorcycle. He may decide not to buy new clothes. Instead, he may choose to save money for the family.

Young fathers should keep relationship issues with the mother separate from the children. Couples argue. They disagree. They should do this when children are not present. Children should not be brought into an argument or used as a threat. Children should never be kept from either parent except if there is mistreatment. Teen parents need to keep their negative feelings about each other from their children. They need to work together to raise healthy children.

Some fathers are legally kept from their children. A father may be asked to stay away from a family if he:
- depends on alcohol or other drugs
- mistreats or is violent to the mother or children
- sexually or verbally mistreats the mother or children

Fathers who pose risks to a family can be dangerous. It is important for these fathers to find help and heal.

The Importance of Fathers

Dads play an important role in the lives of their children. Fathers can be good role models for young boys. Caring fathers teach boys nurturing skills. They show them peaceful ways to solve problems. They pass on special skills learned from their own parents.

Fathers can also model how men act in relationships. Young children observe their father's behaviors. These observations affect how children act in future relationships. A healthy relationship with their father can help children choose other healthy relationships.

Child Development

Each baby is unique, or one of a kind. Fathers can build a bond with the baby as they learn about this special person.

It is important for both young parents to understand child development. For example, babies cry for many reasons. Crying is their only form of communication. This can be hard for parents. They may not know exactly why the baby is crying.

Sometimes a father doesn't know what is wrong with the baby. Still, it is important to try to comfort the baby. Babies like quiet talk and gentle touch. They also like to be held and comforted.

Babies may not do what fathers expect. This sometimes can frustrate fathers. They may not have as much experience with children as the mother does. In North America, many young women baby-sit. Because of this experience, young women usually are expected to understand child development. Therefore, mothers often are the one expected to raise the child.

Responsible Parenting

Part of responsible parenting is learning to be patient with children. Good fathers know their job is to teach. They know never to spank a child in anger. Spanking is an angry response to a child. It teaches children to be violent. Babies should never be spanked.

Parents need to be responsible to set up a safe house for babies and toddlers. Electrical outlets, matches, and candles are found in most homes. These things are dangerous to small children. These threats to the safety of young children should be removed. Young children need to know about existing dangers. They need parents who provide a safe home for them to explore.

Parents who work together value their children. They realize that working together benefits children. It gives children an opportunity to grow up with two important relationships. This happens when parents work as a team.

Points to Consider

How was teen pregnancy dealt with in the 1950s?

What are the benefits when at least two people raise a baby?

Describe different ways parents work together, even when they don't live together.

How does understanding child development make someone a better father?

Chapter Overview

Teen fathers work hard to make the best of their new role. They find a good support system. They finish school.

Teen fathers provide for their families. They get job training or schooling so they can support their families.

Young dads make decisions about their sexuality. Some choose not to have sex or to postpone it. Others use methods to prevent another pregnancy.

Fathers need to work with the mother. This can be difficult. Parents who work as a team put their children first.

Fathers make commitments to their children. This is a benefit to children. It also is healthy for the father.

Chapter 8

Your Future—
Making It Work for You

Teen fathering doesn't stop your life. It simply changes it. Many young men have raised themselves and their children. Their positive choices helped their children. These fathers knew they couldn't change the past. They made the most of the present.

Young fathers need good mentors, or people with experience. Mentors share their experience with young fathers to help them learn something new. Adult men have many experiences to offer a teen father. They can provide support for a new dad. Mentors can help guide young fathers as they parent.

My neighbor, Vince, was at the hospital when Ashley was born. He helped us find a cheap apartment in a good neighborhood. Vince has been around all my life. My father was never around.

Jonas, Age 18

I guess Vince has been the best father to me. I go to him for advice about jobs. He helps me deal with my girlfriend. He encouraged me to start college. I finished my first quarter last week. I don't know how good I would be as a father without him around.

Finish School—It Pays Off

A good education can help you be a better parent. The first step is to finish high school. There are many options after high school. You must decide on the best choice for you.

Job training comes in many forms. Choosing job training can be a hard decision but not a permanent one. Full-time work can be stressful. Some jobs are dangerous. It is important to match your skills and interests.

Fathers have always had a primary role in supporting the family. This has changed in the last 30 years. Today it is more common for both parents to work and support the family. In fact, some fathers stay home to raise the family today.

Should I Stop Having Sex?

Teen parents must make decisions about sexuality. Each decision is personal. Couples must decide which form of pregnancy prevention is best. Some people decide to abstain from sex. They choose not to have sex to prevent future pregnancies.

There are many options for pregnancy prevention. Some options are listed in the table on the next page.

Pregnancy Prevention Options

Nonprescription

1 Male condom—A thin latex or polyurethane covering that fits over the penis to catch sperm. Most effective when used with a spermicide. Also protects against sexually transmitted diseases.

2 Female condom—A bag-like piece of polyurethane that fits inside the vagina. Helps to prevent pregnancy by keeping sperm out of the uterus. Also protects against sexually transmitted diseases.

3 Spermicide—A foam, cream, tablet, or gel put into the vagina to kill sperm. When used correctly together, condoms and spermicides are 97 percent effective in preventing pregnancy.

Prescription

1 Birth control pills—A daily pill that prevents an egg from being released each month.

2 Progestin—A drug given to a woman to prevent an egg from being released each month. Progestin can be given in the form of pills, as a shot, or implanted under the skin.

3 Emergency contraceptive pill (morning after pill)—A combination of tablets that provides emergency birth control when used immediately after unprotected sex or within 72 hours. This is not meant to be an ongoing birth control method. It will not work if implantation of the fertilized egg has occurred.

4 Diaphragm—A rubber cup placed over the cervix to keep sperm out of the uterus. Must be used with a spermicide and a male condom.

Charmaine and I had a baby when I was **Dimitris, Age 20** 16. I had been with girls for about four years. I started having sex in seventh grade. I never thought about pregnancy. My girlfriends talked about it, though. They were way more scared about it. Now I'm the one who is scared. It's been hard. I had to quit school and get a job. Charmaine and I aren't dating anymore. I'm not seeing anybody. I'm not having sex or nothing. I'm just trying to help raise my baby.

Preventing Future Pregnancies

Consistent use of a birth control method to prevent pregnancy is important. Most methods work well if used correctly. Instructions are included with methods that are purchased. A doctor can suggest different methods. Many couples talk about the best method for them. Responsible couples who are sexually active talk about parenting and pregnancy prevention.

Teen fathering is a serious job. A second child would double the expenses. Some fathers have a second child with a different woman. This is hard on the children. Fathers have to deal with two different homes. Parents who plan a second pregnancy use careful thought. Pregnancy prevention allows parents to plan when and if a second child will be added to the family.

Cooperative Fathers and Mothers

A father needs to work with the mother. This is not always easy. A mother may try to keep a father from his baby. There are reasons why this happens. Sometimes the father may be abusing drugs. Some fathers may hit the mother or the child. Often, the government steps in if this happens. It will help keep the father away until he is healthy again.

Parents should work as a team. This works best when both parents are healthy. This means both are physically and emotionally ready to parent. They put the child's needs first. They talk about how they will raise the child. They compromise. Good fathers learn to separate issues about the mother from the child.

Teen Fathers Who Commit

Good fathers commit to their children. They are involved. They spend time with the baby. They provide money for the baby's needs. They learn how their child develops.

Responsible fathers teach many things to children. They love and nurture children. They play with them. They are good role models. They read to their children and model a love of learning.

Good fathers also help themselves. They know when to take breaks. They value the mother, even if the two of them no longer date. Good fathers finish school and get job training. Some attend college. They find a support system for themselves. A healthy dad is a benefit to a child. Teen fatherhood is a challenge. Many young dads learn to meet the challenge. Their children love them for it.

Points to Consider

Why do teen fathers need a mentor? What are the benefits of having one?

What steps would you take to prepare yourself for a job?

Why is it important for teen fathers to prevent a second pregnancy?

How do children benefit from a father's commitment?

Glossary

biological father (bye-oh-LOG-i-kuhl FAH-thur)—the man who creates a child from his sperm

child support (CHILDE suh-PORT)—money paid by a parent to support a child

communication (kuh-MYOO-nuh-KAY-shuhn)—a process of sharing information

conception (kuhn-SEP-shuhn)—union of a male sperm with a female egg to form a human being

fetus (FEE-tuhss)—an unborn, developing human being

hormone (HOR-mohn)—a chemical that controls a bodily function

immunization (IM-yuh-nye-zay-shuhn)—a shot that makes the body able to resist certain diseases

intercourse (IN-tur-korss)—physical sexual contact between people that involves the genitals

legal custody (LEE-guhl KUHSS-tuh-dee)—the right to make decisions about a child

partnership (PART-nur-ship)—two or more people who work together for a common goal

paternity (puh-TUR-nuh-tee)—being a father

physical custody (fiz-uh-kuhl KUHSS-tuh-dee)—responsibility for daily care of a child

prenatal care (pree-NAY-tuhl KAIR)—a pregnant woman's regular doctor visits before a baby is born

For More Information

Ayer, Eleanor H. *Everything You Need to Know About Teen Fatherhood*. New York: Rosen, 1995.

Brott, Armin A., and Jennifer Ash. *The Expectant Father: Facts, Tips, and Advice for Dads-to-Be*. New York: Pocket Books, 1993.

Cosby, Bill. *Fatherhood*. New York: Berkley, 1994.

Endersbe, Julie K. *Teen Pregnancy: Tough Choices*. Mankato, MN: Capstone Press, 2000.

Lang, Paul S., and Susan S. Lang. *Teen Fathers*. New York: Franklin Watts, 1995.

Useful Addresses and Internet Sites

Alan Guttmacher Institute
120 Wall Street
New York, NY 10005
www.agi-usa.org

American Coalition for Fathers and Children
22365 El Toro Road, #335
Lake Forest, CA 92630
1-800-978-DADS
www.acfc.org

Dads Can
St. Mary's Annex, Room 411
London, ON N6A 1Y6
CANADA
1-888-DADS-CAN
www.dadscan.org

Fathers' Resource Center
430 Oak Grove Street, Suite B3
Minneapolis, MN 55403
frc@slowlane.com

National Center on Fathers and Families
University of Pennsylvania
3700 Walnut Street, Box 58
Philadelphia, PA 19104-6216
http://www.ncoff.gse.upenn.edu/

Dads at a Distance
www.daads.com
Encourages fathers who have to be away from
their children

The Fatherhood Project
www.fatherhoodproject.org/
Education project supporting men's
involvement in child rearing

FatherNet
www.cyfc.umn.edu/FatherNet
A national program encouraging father
involvement

National Fatherhood Initiative
www.fatherhood.org
Current information on increasing father
involvement

Index